TABLE OF CONTENTS

I0409911

List of Figures

Weather Operation: White Carpet

The strike package is a complicated mixture of fourth and fifth generation aircraft, integrated with ISR and strike unmanned aerial vehicles (UAV). The lead element into the area of regard (AOR) is a set of strike UAV's. As the unmanned aircraft enter the threat areas, the enemy integrated air defense system (IADS) becomes fully active. The ability to engage the strike package is limited to kinetic surface to air missiles (SAM) and anti-aircraft artillery (AAA). Sophisticated directed energy weapons (DEWs) attempt to engage but are thwarted by a cloud layer between the strike aircraft and the ground. The unmanned vehicles make short work of the kinetic systems, essentially following the guidance and infra-red (IR) signatures of the launch sites. As the UAV's descend below the cloud layer enroute to their SAM and AAA targets, some are intercepted by DE systems. Only three of 120 aircraft are engaged, indicating the severe degradation of the enemy's IADS.

The manned fighters and bombers enter the AOR with a reduced threat array and ability to focus on the enemy's less-capable fighter defenses. After disposing of enemy fighters and avoiding or evading kinetic surface to air weapons, each aircraft delivers their deadly payload. The return to base is nearly as smooth. The enemy relied excessively on DEW defense systems. The fear of nearly zero time of flight (TOF) DE IADS was rendered totally ineffective by that mysterious cloud layer.

Operations actually began six hours prior to the strike aircraft entering the AOR. The CFACC directed Weather Control to proceed with operations. A Global Hawk was on station at high altitude and 150 miles "upstream" from the AOR. At the determined altitude and location, the UAV released its balloon payload. Diamond nano-skinned balloons of approximately three to five millimeters in diameter began distributing through approximately every square meter in a pre-determined column. Upon command, solar cells and elemental mirrors in the balloons began to absorb sunlight, heating the skin of the balloon. The entire column, controlled through the balloon sensor and actor network (SANET), began to heat and develop into a localized high pressure area. As the high pressure developed, the jet stream was pushed north of the AOR, stabilizing the atmosphere between the forward edge of the battle area (FEBA) and primary target area. More UAVs launched from near the FEBA hours prior were established in their assigned orbits. On command, similar diamond balloons were released, reporting current localized temperature, water vapor content and pressure back to the UAVs. As the UAVs passed their data back to Weather Control, computers developed specific inputs to the atmospheric equation. These inputs were sent back to the balloons. Some balloons utilized electrolysis to remove water molecules in the atmosphere. Others gathered water molecules to build cloud condensation nuclei as they maneuvered towards their desired altitude. Some balloons heated or cooled, to establish a temperature/pressure ratio allowing for the formation of clouds. Over the course of a few hours a definite cloud deck developed, constantly supported by an artificial high pressure area and fed by an army of micro balloons networked, powered and operated by nanotechnology.

During the mass brief of the strike aircraft, Intelligence described the lethal matrix of directed energy IADS in the AOR. After the aircrew reviewed their routes in reference to the threats, the Defensive Weather Controller (DWC) began his brief of DE denial: A cloud deck from 11,000 to 12,000 ft mean sea level (MSL). The DWC estimated that any optical and microwave systems will be rendered ineffective. Even with the destruction of the delivery/networking UAV's, the generated weather phenomenon was expected to last approximately four hours with a 97% match to briefed description. Potential for external weather interference was mitigated by a preemptive high pressure; jet stream steering trough established 120 nm north of the AOR. All sensors reported positive generated condensation with confirmation from optical satellite feeds. A young F-35 wingman whispered to his flight lead during the brief, "Man, I hope this weather stuff works."

Introduction

Directed Energy is fast becoming the popular weapon of the future. Along these lines, optical intelligence is still, and will remain to be a critical method of targeting weapons. These weapons will be wide-spread by approximately 2010.[1] The United States needs to incorporate the defense against these weapons with the same intensity used developing anti-ballistic missile defenses. One of the major drawbacks to optical or directed energy systems is the inability to effectively penetrate clouds or dense fog. Advances in technology are beginning to bring weather phenomena more completely under our control. Greatly increased computing power and miniaturized delivery systems will allow us to create specific perturbations in local atmospheric conditions. These perturbations allow for the immediate and persistent ability to create localized fog or stratus cloud formations shielding critical assets against attack from energy based weapons. The future of nanotechnology will enable creation of stratus cloud formations to defeat DEW and optically targeted attacks on United Sates assets. Focus on weather control in an isolated defensive manner helps to alleviate the fear of widespread destruction on non-military personnel and property.

The overall solution to this weather creation problem involves networked miniature balloons feeding and receiving data from a four-dimensional variation (4d-Var) computer model through a sensor and actor network. A network of diamond-walled balloons enters the area to be changed and then both measures and affects localized temperature and vapor content. This system effectively shortens the control loop of an atmospheric system to the point it can be "managed." The capabilities in the diamond-walled balloons are based on the future of nanotechnology.

Methodology

Determining weather control methods in the year 2030 required the use of multiple methodologies. The question of "What is required to control the weather and how do we do it?" needed an answer. The entire process began with an extensive environmental scan. Current methods of weather modification were studied to determine limitations in weather control. This step also involved finding key experts in the fields related to weather control. An initial concept relevance diagram was developed. Two individuals help assemble a panel of experts. The Public Information Chairman of Weather Modification Association (WMA) and contract manager of multiple National Oceanic and Atmospheric Administration (NOAA) programs, Dr. Thomas DeFelice, and Mr. Peter Backlund, Director of Research at the National Center for Atmospheric Research (NCAR) helped establish contacts to develop requirements for an initial concept diagram. The concept diagram was then vetted among the experts and a community of weather modification researchers and entrepreneurs at WMA (www.weathermodification.org). The concept relevance tree was refined (Appendix A) to the specific requirements to create an opaque mesocale stratus cloud formation – that which would be useful on the battlefield. Experts from weather modeling, weather system dynamics and nanotechnology helped link requirements to capabilities. These links were developed into a component relevance diagram (Appendix B). Dr. Ross Hoffman from Atmospheric and Environmental Research Inc provided guidance on weather simulation, systems and dynamics. Dr. J. Storrs Hall, author of *Nanofuture,* and research fellow at the Institute for Molecular Manufacturing, supported research on nanotechnology. Concurrently, the author conducted an environmental scan in the area of smart networks and military application of weather control technology.

The roadmap for this discussion of operational weather control involves a discussion of requirements, application and capabilities. The conversation begins with the capability of weather to interfere or deny optical targeting and DEW attacks. The discussion then explains the complexity of weather and system control concepts. A relevance tree with direct input from field specific experts flushes out the intricacies of these technologies and their dependencies on each other. Finally, the future of these technologies is discussed to place weather control in the 2030 timeframe.

Problem Significance

Weather control opens vast opportunities for the United States military to explore. Besides enabling many operations, a key capability involves the defense against future optical targeting and directed energy threats. A simple opaque cloud of water vapor negates the optical tracking and engagement of a target with directed energy. While controlling the atmosphere over a target area is far more difficult than setting the temperature with an air conditioner, advances in technology will make it possible for men to shape weather conditions in a localized area. When we harness the clouds and the fog, we can use it as a shield against offensive capabilities in 2030.

For current precision weapons to be effective, the target must be found, fixed, tracked, attacked and assessed.[2] Water vapor in the form of fog or layered cloud formations causes a problem for these capabilities. Many systems require visual or infrared (IR) detection and tracking methods for adequate resolution. If the target is moving, weapons are continuously guided by designated the target with lasers. Directed energy weapons turn the laser itself into the

5

weapon. Other methods of detection and tracking include millimeter and microwave detection. All of these methods of applying DE to target engagement can be thwarted by the mighty water droplet.[3] There are methods (varying wavelengths) and power levels of DE that can penetrate weather for targeting purposes, but the power and close-range required exposes them to direct attack.[4]

A few issues have re-ignited weather control and modification interests. Increased computer modeling power has made detailed experimentation possible. The fear of global warming and increased publicity of weather related tragedies have ignited the sciences. The technology of weather modification has expanded into rain or snow development (cloud seeding), hail dissipation and lightning dissipation. Current credible scientific study deals with hurricane, tornado and flood mitigation.[5] China is the current lead investor in weather modification and control technology, investing nearly 40 million dollars annually.[6] The Chinese efforts were put on display for the world during the 2008 Summer Olympics.[7] The efforts of the Chinese to reduce the amount of rain (by inducing precipitation elsewhere) *seemed* to work, but as is a current issue with weather modification, there is not indisputable proof. The military uses of controlling the weather are vast, and future technology will enable more specific control of the weather – actually creating, not modifying weather.

Others in the United States Air Force have forecasted the ability to use weather as a tactical advantage. The Air Force 2025 paper *Weather as a Force Multiplier: Owning the Weather in 2025* specifically addresses the increase in computing power in conjunction with current weather modification techniques to shape the battlespace. Pressing this an additional 10 years into the future will see more dynamic and specific use of nano and micro technologies in conjunction with increased autonomous networking capability. Rather than steering a storm or moving fog, a military commander will create weather to utilize defensively.

6

Defeating Optical Target Engagement and Directed Energy

To engage a moving target, a system must detect and track the target in real-time. Then, a weapon must be guided or updated with the targets location during the weapons time of flight. Finally, the weapon must survive the flight through the atmosphere, on the way to the target. It must be understood how effective weather is against DEWs and optical target engagement on the battlefield. Weather affects deliverable through the technology in this discussion begins above 1,000 feet above ground level (AGL), avoiding turbulent interaction with the ground.[8] The weather phenomena to be used as a DEW defeat mechanism is established as a stratus or alto-stratus layer of clouds comprised of a mixture of crystals and droplets of water.[9] This cloud is as thick as required to be optically opaque against visible, infrared (IR) and ultraviolet (UV) wavelengths. An approximate cloud thickness of 300 to 500 feet is assumed, resulting in a visibly opaque cloud formation.[10] Actual cloud thicknesses will depend on results from computer modeling and inputs of cloud vapor content (crystal, vapor and micro-droplets) as well as predicted weapons to defeat. A discussion of optical engagement and targeting will show how clouds can force the enemy into alternate and attackable means of surveillance. Second, a discussion of future DEW technology and limitations will show how clouds will reduce DE effectiveness for strategic and tactical use.

Optical Target Engagement

Optical tracking and targeting can be accomplished by a variety of means. Methods range from ground based outposts to satellites in orbit. There are three distinct capabilities of finding, tracking and guiding weapons. Finding, tracking and guiding weapons on a target are capabilities that are dependent on the detail you can see, the time available to see the target and the method you are using to update a weapon in flight. The ability to simply find a target is the least complicated, if it doesn't move!

The higher the altitude at which an optical platform operates generally results in reduced flexibility of its search area. Military targeting satellites would have similar requirements as civilian satellites such as GEOEYE 1. GEOEYE 1 operates in the region of low earth orbit and can produce 16 inch resolutions with an approximate seven foot positional accuracy.[11] Lower earth orbit is roughly considered to be 200 to 930 miles above the earth.[12] At this resolution you can identify types of vehicles and objects while determining coordinates upon which to have weapons or energy impact. The limitation involves time. GEOEYE-1 is a comparable civilian system which can revisit a location approximately every two days.[13] If the target is visible and does not move during the two day envelope, then systems such as GEOEYE-1 can effectively maintain a track. Systems like GEOEYE-1 cannot penetrate weather phenomena that the naked eye cannot see through. Optical occlusion for more than two days can be accomplished by weather phenomena that deny acquisition of the ground. The effect of this denial drives the enemy to utilize a system closer to the target area, denying the current sanctuary of space or requiring a different method of surveillance. Alternate methods of surveillance will require an electromagnetic method outside of passive visual, IR, UV detection and surveillance closer to the target area. Electromagnetic methods require the transmission of energy, resulting in the pinpointing of and possible destruction of the transmitting source. Reducing the range to the area of interest exposes the manned or unmanned optical targeting platform to attack from the target area.

Optically tracking and targeting are similar in concept with the exception of time. Dynamic targets and precision weapons require a method to update both target location and weapon flight path throughout the weapon time of flight. Without transmitting electromagnetic energy, optical systems are required to provide the resolution and tracking capability for accurate engagement of most target types. Atmospheric moisture that is thick enough to occlude the target or the target's movement effectively negates both optical tracking and laser-based methods of guiding weapons.[14] By creating clouds in specific locations and altitude blocks, optical weapons systems will be forced to occupy predictable locations making them easier to target or avoid. Making the tracking laser and weapon the same thing reduces weapon time of flight and is a critical capability of DE.

Directed Energy Weapons

High Energy Lasers (HEL) and High Power Microwaves (HPM) are currently the primary methods of directed energy attack. Both of these categories break down further into the methods of creating the laser or microwave energy as well as transmission and control of the beams. It is the expectation that within the next 15 years, these types of DEW will become increasingly common on the battlefield.[15] Department of Defense (DOD) interest in directed energy programs spans from the tactical to strategic uses on the ground and in space.[16] HEL and HPM technologies have different methods of effectiveness on their target. HELs apply high temperatures on the surface, destroying their target. Lasers can also cause disorienting effects on the operator of their target.[17] HPMs affect the internal circuitry of the target or internal tissues of the operators.[18] Both HELs and HPMs have the strengths of zero time of flight but the effects require a great deal of energy to remain coherent from the weapon to the target. HEL and HPM require separate discussion of effects and defeat mechanisms.

DEWs have a limit of operation within the electromagnetic spectrum. The power of these weapons depends on their electromagnetic signature. Figure 1 shows where laser and microwave weapons inhabit the electromagnetic spectrum. Both wavelength and frequency are tied together since the speed of the energy weapon is considered to be constant at the speed of light (c). As a result, the variables of wavelength or frequency are characteristics that can be modified. The amount of energy per second, measured as watts, depends on the pulse length or total amount of lasing or radiating time for a given beam. As frequency increases, wavelength decreases and the amount of energy in a directed beam also increases.

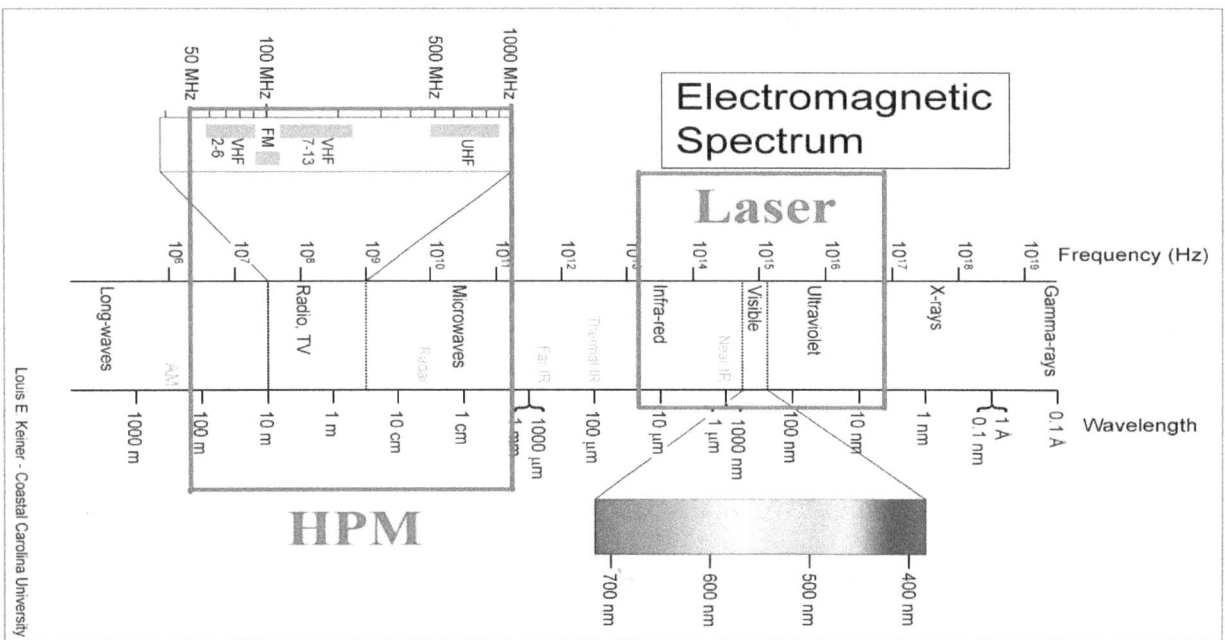

Figure 1. The Directed Energy Weapons in the Electromagnetic Spectrum (adaped from http://kingfish.coastal.edu/marine/animations courtesy of Louis Keiner).

$$\text{Energy} = \text{Plank's constant} \times \text{Frequency}$$
$$E = h\nu = hc/\lambda$$
$$\text{Where } h = \text{Plank's constant is } 6.626 \times 10^{-34} \text{ joules per second}$$
$$\lambda = \text{wavelength}$$

This is important because longer wavelengths have the best chance of surviving an encounter with particles in their way.[19] In the region of one micrometer (1μm) wavelengths, directed energy can survive interaction with water vapor but still do not have the energy density to overcome atmospheric absorption.[20] A trade off is made between getting a specific amount of energy over a long range or having a lower amount of energy survive interaction with weather. As the wavelength increases, the weapon must be closer in range and operate for a longer

10

amount of time to deliver an effective density of electromagnetic energy. This is where the defeat of DEW due to weather occurs.

Ground based HEL systems may be used against airborne and space based targets. Space and airborne lasers can be employed against fielded maneuver forces as well as strategic locations such as governmental facilities, headquarters, and operations centers.[21] In both cases, the laser "beam" must travel through the atmosphere to the target. The future of laser technology is expected to produce approximately 10 million watts by the year 2030.[22] At this power level the contact area of an aircraft's aluminum skin can exceed 1500° F within a second, causing its destruction.[23] Laser weapons require approximately a second of target tracking time, nearly negating the requirement to continuously track a target. Superheating the target requires getting the laser to the target. With the exception of space to space employment of lasers, the beam energy must travel through the earth's atmosphere. Lasers have to deal with refraction, reflection and absorption during their short time of flight.

In the absence of clouds, the laser still must account for diffraction issues due to varying densities at the propagation medium.[24] The beam of light may not arrive at the intended target due to bending caused by temperature and density changes in air. To help overcome this, laser weapons systems utilize a secondary compensation and tracking laser to evaluate the atmosphere enroute to the target. Data from the tracking laser continuously compensates for the atmosphere by changing characteristics and aiming of the main destructive beam. This tracking laser has much less power with a long wavelength to penetrate atmospheric turbulence. This targeting laser, however, suffers from the same issues as current kinetic weapon lasing systems; the inability to penetrate water vapor that is opaque to visible light. Before the weapon is even employed, it is defeated by opaque water vapor.

The coherent electromagnetic energy used as the weapon in HELs suffers from loss due to refraction, reflection and absorption. Refraction reduces the light beam focus and coherency. The intensity of power is reduced as optical properties of water droplets and ice crystals bend the laser beam, breaking it into smaller elements of coherent light.[25] The thicker the cloud layer, the more the beam is refracted. Reflection also scatters the beam by bouncing portions of the laser out of the direction of travel. The reflection in clouds reduces the intensity and power of the beam for each element of the cloud it interacts with. A 100 foot thick stratus cloud of mixed ice and droplet particles can totally obscure a laser, reducing it to a glimmer of incoherent light with negligible heating effect beyond the clouds.[26] The total power, intensity and coherence of the beam will determine whether it can "burn through" the cloud and have any applicable energy on the far side of the cloud. Keep in mind, the targeting and compensation laser has already been defeated so we do not know if the weapon energy is correctly aimed at target. Can a laser tunnel through the cloud with enough energy?

The concept of using a terawatt tunneling pulse laser has been suggested to give a DE laser a path through clouds. This concept has a problem with the other issues of atmospheric absorption due to water phase changes. The concept requires a continuous wave and pulsed laser to coexist in a coaxial fashion. The pulsed laser punches a hole in the cloud as the continuous wave laser propagates unhindered.[27] The theory works when tested against homogenous water vapor aerosols.[28] However, everything changes when the cloud is a mix of ice, droplets and vapor. As the laser heats the mixture, the aerosol and ice form a combination of regionalized vapor and plasma. The tunneling and primary lasers now have to deal with the absorption of energy from the changing aerosol with the addition of plasma.[29] Both lasers themselves have an excessively chaotic effect on the non-homogenous cloud, further dissipating the beams.[30] After the laser passes through the atmosphere, the cloud mixture immediately re-establishes the mixture equilibrium to the pre-laser state.[31] This is the strength of utilizing the mixture of water

phases rather than smart dust or opaque mechanical means to defend against DEW. With enough

power, it is conceivable that a laser or laser combination could eventually burn through a mixture

at the cost of time and power.

HPM weapons attack the electrical or network functionality of a system. HPM can also

have direct effects on personnel. The non-lethal effects of HPM on humans are significant,

occurring at the range of thousands of feet but are negated by any physical structure between the

transmitter and target.[32] The long range capability of HPMs deals with the capability of

disabling electronic components of weapons systems in the kilometers range of effect.[33] This

discussion centers around the projection of electromagnetic pulse (EMP) or associated effects

over a tactical range effecting aircraft and command and control (C2) capabilities.[34] To disable

C2 networks and weapons systems, a microwave source must be projected onto the system under

attack. The difference between HEL and HPM occurs in the frequency/wavelength of

electromagnetic spectrum as well as the size or coherence of the propagated energy. HPM is not

employed in a tight, coherent beam of energy. HPM are "shot" as a broad region of energy

waves. As a result, defeating HPM is less dependent on the reflected and refracted disruption of

coherent excited radiation and more reliant on the absorption broadcast energy. Microwaves

provide a density of energy that can destroy complex electronic devices while still being aimed

at a specific location in space. The position of HPM in the electromagnetic spectrum requires a

large antenna to aim microwave energy.[35] The amount of energy required at the target to

accomplish affects can be considered a constant. Like optical targeting and engagement, the

ability to deliver energy against a target can be made dependent on range due to weather

interference.

To defeat HPM, weather needs to reduce the energy transmitted over range to the point of negligible returns. Beam steering and intensity become primary factors in the delivery of energy. Once again, clouds provide a method of both denying atmospheric sampling and establishment of a homogeneous medium. HPM can penetrate weather, but the use of clouds can limit the effectiveness of HPM to specific regions of frequency for which equipment can be hardened. Microwaves attenuate by imposing most of their energy on water molecules. This is how a microwave oven cooks food. This is the method that clouds can use to lock effective HPM weapons into specific frequencies. The natural attenuations caused by water, nitrogen and carbon monoxide in clouds constrain HPM to frequencies of 22, 35, 94, 140 or 220 GHz.[36] You can effectively, and more cheaply, harden critical equipment against these five frequencies rather than the spectrum of HPM. Attenuation through absorption still occurs in these bands, requiring the HPM source to reduce range to target and increase antenna size to be effective.[37] Weather cannot have much effect on those HPM that involve delivery of EMP devices in close proximity to their target. HPM bombs or EMP generators are intended to function within a kilometer of the target. At these ranges, the delivery system can be targeted by conventional assets.

It is the natural phenomena of refraction, reflection and absorption that clouds enhance in defense of ISTR and DEWs. The abundance of the crystalline, liquid and vapor water in clouds makes them a credible and persistent defense against DEW. Clouds either totally negate the DEW threat or force the enemy into an alternate method of targeting and attack. Creation of the described 1000 foot thick stratus clouds is the challenge for technology.

Weather Control Past and Present

There is a long history of man attempting to control or modify the weather. Most attempts at weather control involved enhancing or utilizing an existing weather phenomenon such as creating rain from already present clouds. Weather dissipation was an interest of the military during the early 1940's, utilizing large trenches of burning fuel to dissipate fog to enable aircraft to takeoff on bomber missions.[38] Later, in the 1960's and 1970's Project Popeye was a military attempt to increase localized rainfall to reduce mobility on the supply routes of North Vietnam, shaping the battlespace for war planners.[39] Concurrently project GROMET II was underway in the Philippine Islands. This project indicated more measurable success in producing rain to stop a severe drought.[40] Since then, the US military dramatically reduced funding for active weather control activities, leaving it to private industries to brighten the hopes of Midwest farmers in search of rain.

Civilian attempts at weather control centered on making existing clouds produce rain. Making rain was intended to help farmers overcome droughts. Additional interest developed in making clouds deteriorate into rain in areas that were not prone to flooding. Seeding clouds could also reduce the severity of storms and hail damage to crops and property. The US Weather Bureau undertook a project of massive cloud seeding in 1947.[41] For the next twenty years, research and experimentation focused on what types of chemicals or methods of seeding could produce precipitation. The research itself was problematic due to the inability to link rainfall results directly to specific variables in the activities of cloud seeding. Variables such as seeding media, cloud type, time of the day and season were changing during the experiments.[42] Two major problems were identified. First, the timeframe and geographic area of measuring was too large, making attribution of seeding methods problematic. Second, the physics of cloud production, sustenance and finally destruction were not understood.[43] [44] The speed at which a system could be identified, seeded and measured for results was too slow. Satellite, radar and remote temperature measurement capabilities eventually helped scientists to quickly identify and evaluate a weather system during an experiment.[45]

New technologies such as radar and satellite sensing have enabled the study of cloud lifecycle dynamics. Lightening suppression, tornado and hurricane detection and dissipation are now being hypothesized.[46] Cloud seeding is still the predominant method of weather modification, requiring an existent weather system. The effects of seeding and the methods of applying them can now be measured, directly attributing results to system variables.[47] It was technology leaps in measurement that allowed scientists to accurately determine the variables and results of a system over a broad geographic and time span. The ongoing leap in weather forecasting and control research is based on computer power and modeling.

Computing power and modeling developments have allowed weather scientists to forecast complex weather systems effectively. Downstream forecasting, estimating when an upstream weather system will arrive, has given way to accurately determining multiple weather system interactions. The Weather Research and Forecasting Model (WRFM) is the current mesoscale weather prediction model based on three dimensional variation (3d-Var).[48] The accuracy of the modeling system depends on the stability of the variables and the computing power used by the model. The combination of this powerful modeling capability and real-time data available from measuring devices allows this model to forecast the birth and lifecycle of a weather system.[49]

The strength of the WRFM rests in the use of nonhydrostatic atmospheric modeling.[50] This method allows for the model to simulate non-linear chaos within clouds and systems of clouds. This is important because now a model can extrapolate an output from a system that is not proportional to the inputs. The WRFM applies the interaction of small-scale and mesoscale systems in the area of five to thousands of kilometers, dependent on the ability to accurately measure these areas. The WRFM is an initial step towards removing the stigma of applying Chaos Theory towards mesoscale weather systems. A system is broken down into elements.

16

The size of these predicted elements only depends on the frequency of measurement and number of data points available in the given system. The WRFM does not look at the global system, it does accurately simulate the internal and intrasystem physics of clouds.[51] So why can't the weatherman get it right?

The availability of the WRFM and the computing power to support it are limited. The WRFM is a collaborative operation between the NOAA, NCAR and six other major organizations. The WRFM is mostly used for research and future forecast method modeling. Getting the proper amount and timeliness of data into the WRFM is the weatherman's limitation. Most radar and satellite measurement methods take samples of portions of a weather system. Updating and maintaining a persistent stream of system data from distinct points in the system simultaneously is difficult. Most current methods of measurement are very capable of describing portions of a weather system by their movement or change. This method of mass flux element measurement works well with linear models; inputs are proportional to outputs. The non-linear modeling requires for selective use of data. For better data assimilation and utilization, the measurement devices almost need to be a part of the weather system, and this is where technology will fill the gap. The fast modeling and computations of the WRFM are now hindered by the accuracy of measuring in the system. How does one go from taking accurate forecasting to the actual development of a weather system?

Foundations of Weather Control

Relevance Tree

Relevance trees helps break a concept down to basic functions and requirement. For weather control, these topics further devolve into the physical or operational parts of a system to create a cloud in the atmosphere. The relevance tree was used as a tool to determine what technologies need to be linked in order to control a complex system like weather. Through collaboration between experts in weather, computer modeling, and nanotechnologies, the elements of the system are reduced from required functions to the suggested components for weather creation.

The concept relevance tree (Appendix A) presents cloud development requirements with some additional considerations. Isolating and establishing the atmospheric area to be modified became the initial area of discussion among members of the Weather Modification Association and subject matter experts (SMEs). The concept tree indicated a grand set of ten major criteria:[52]

1. Establish/Isolate a System
2. Measure Variables in System
3. Determine Required Variable Values in the System
4. Change Variables in the System
5. Network System Components
6. Control Location of Components
7. Deconfliction With other Assets
8. Manpower
9. Side Effects
10. Vulnerability to Attack
(Weather Modification Association panel of experts and the author, 2008)

The size of the problem required the researcher to focus the problem to just accomplishing the development of a cloud system. As a result, items eight through ten were removed from this project. Manpower, possible side effects and vulnerability of the weather control system are important but were found to be beyond the scope of this project. The remaining items were further broken down to the descriptions of their function. Great consideration was given to the difficulty of isolating the atmosphere for modeling. Debate and expert input settled the issue to broad effects stabilizing the mass flow to manageable levels in which the elements within the mesoscale could be affected would suffice. The concept relevance tree has been broken down to the critical requirements of isolating an atmospheric area; measuring and setting variables within the system.

A closed loop system needs to be developed to control weather. Weather control goes one step further than the current capabilities of 3d-Var modeling while measuring atmospheric variables outside the system. Two major technological humps stand in the way of weather control. First, making a cloud in a specified geographic area requires setting and isolating a system to create weather in. Much like "controlling the air mass" with an air conditioner. Second, the actual methods of altering the temperature, pressure, or vapor content within the elements of the system.

The Ideal Gas Law, PV=nRT is an extremely simplistic way of regarding the control of weather. Water vapor content changes this from an ideal gas equation, but sufficiently models the interaction. Cloud development depends on vapor content and method of coalescing into an opaque cloud.

$$\text{Pressure X Volume = Quantity (moles) X Gas constant X Temperature}$$

$$PV = nRT$$

Condensation rate is proportional to vapor condensation based on the Ideal Gas Law. It is the iterative and complex interaction between the equilibrium of condensation and the Ideal Gas Law that will develop clouds. Volume, in this case, depends on mass flow rates. Pressure and temperature are dependent on each other and the water content in the air will determine at what temperature/pressure a cloud will form. The nuclei of cloud formations can vary from water droplets to micro ice-crystals. The change in pressure and temperature with altitude determine the construct of that mixture. How do you control the inputs and outputs to your system?

I Give You Nanotechnology!

The component relevance tree (Appendix B) matched the requirements. Cross-referencing the requirements with the environmental scan of future nanotechnology and computer modeling provided solutions to the concept relevance tree. The primary problem determined through the relevance diagram was speed and precision at which a closed-loop weather control system could operate. Nanotechnology enabled sensors and networks answered the problems of measuring, altering and communicating the variables within a weather system. 4d-Var modeling combined with current computing power and accurate data accounted for the control of the system. The delivery of these systems can be accomplished with current technology. Having the sensors, network and means of modification of the atmosphere part of the proposed cloud system removes control lag. The center of this weather control system revolves around a formation of diamond nano-skinned balloons encasing a host of nanomachines.

Current weather modification research focuses on the new concept of determining critical optimal perturbations in atmospheric conditions that will, in essence "box in" a volume of airspace.[53] The area of interest does not need to have zero mass flow. The flow only needs to be stabilized and directional enough to allow for modification of temperature, pressure and vapor content to the degree that it results in cloud formations. Perturbations can be as simple as heating or cooling a large area of atmosphere. Large space-based reflectors could quickly generate a large high pressure area. The perturbation does not need to be as specific as building a cloud system and may be hundreds of miles away from the area of interest.[54] Once these designed blockades are in effect, the air mass that has been stabilized can then be adjusted. This is similar to using smoke in test section of a wind-tunnel. The flow only needs to be constant and directional enough for the smoke added to allow for visualization of aerodynamic effects in the tunnel test section.

Micro and nanotechnology provide both a detailed sensor grid to measure critical variables in a weather generation algorithm and then fill in the variables required to generate the desired effects. Current computer power enables 4d-Var modeling. Computing power in 2020 will enable the networking and sensor grid required 4d-Var analysis to determine variable settings to establish these perturbations to control the system.[55] 4d-Var extrapolates on the capabilities of WRFM 3d-Var analysis and determines the minimum large scale perturbation necessary.[56] The modeling starts with small initial state perturbations and simulates the non-linear response over a 6 or 12 hour window.[57] Future applications of these perturbations take the form of isolated low and high pressure areas or troughs to steer the jet stream or its affect in relation to the area of interest. Making the high or low pressure area can be as simple as heating or cooling a massive column of air with diamond balloons.[58] Experiments on 4d-Var modeling began in 2002, already capable of handing weather control data. Dr. Hoffman of Atmospheric and Environmental Research Incorporated and the former NASA Institute for Advanced Concepts (NAIC), denies that weather is a truly chaotic system when modeled through 4d-Var methods.[59]

Once the mass flow into and out of an area is controlled, it becomes a simple issue of establishing specific localized temperature (dew point spread), pressure gradient and water content per volume of air through a column in the atmosphere. Dr. J. Storrs Hall provided a solution to half of the concept relevance tree through insight on diamond nano-skinned balloons. The component tree helps indicate now nanotechnology will enable diamond nano-skin balloons to accomplish several tasks. Dr. Hall best describes the diamond balloons.

> "You build a little balloon, my guess is the balloon needs to be somewhere between a millimeter and a centimeter in size. It has a very thin shell of diamond, maybe just a nanometer thick. It is round, and it has inside it an equatorial plane that is a mirror. If you squished it flat, you would only have a few nanometers thick of material. Although you could build a balloon out of materials that we build balloons out of now, it would not be economical for what I'm going to use it for."[60]

21

Motion, location and networking of the balloons can be controlled in several ways. Altitude is controlled through the buoyancy of the balloon through a combination of electrolysis of water and nano-pumps removing molecular water from within the balloon. The walls of the balloon could have nano-fans, providing additional thrust.[61, 62] Utilization of the earth's magnetic field and the charge on the skin of the balloons themselves will aid in formation keeping with other balloons.[63] Nano-network controllers within each balloon will maintain contact with neighboring balloons. Solar power through the nano-antenna arrays will charge nano-batteries.[64] Proton exchange membrane (PEM) batteries are current day nanotechnology that is powered by electrolysis of water.[65] Directional micro-antenna will be able to determine position of the balloons with the formation relative to one another. The diamond balloons will house an array of sensor and communication technology which is currently being developed to build radios from carbon nanotubes.[66] These communication systems collect and transmit onsite, accurate data to the complex computer systems that model and establish the controls for a weather system. Some of the larger balloons function as a node, housing a GPS receiver[67] and micronized network uplink to provide high frequency communication of the network to a ground station or UAV.[68] The distribution of these balloons will depend on the amount of atmospheric mass flow in the AOR. Discussions with WMA participants and Dr. Hall estimate at least one to two balloons per cubic meter would be required to initiate changes in conditions. These estimates were based on current cloud seeding densities. Networking these balloons is similar to current research into nano-swarms.

The study of sensor and actor networks (SANET) encompasses the communication, control and activity of our proposed balloon network. Such a network concept includes the requirement to maneuver nodes and communicate in a complex and distributed network.[69] The study of self controlling and communicating networks began in the 1960s.[70] The concept accelerated within the last five years with the spread of integrated wireless networking.[71] The

function of SANETs specifically requires a network of sensors to communicate, maintain

positional distribution and sense among a distribution of nodes.[72] These nodes then pass the data

to and from a monolithic processing center, our 4d-Var model in this case. SANETs are

currently limited by architecture and power, but are already being developed.[73] The weather

control application of such networks follows the development timeline and technology of

Autonomous Nanotechnology Swarms.

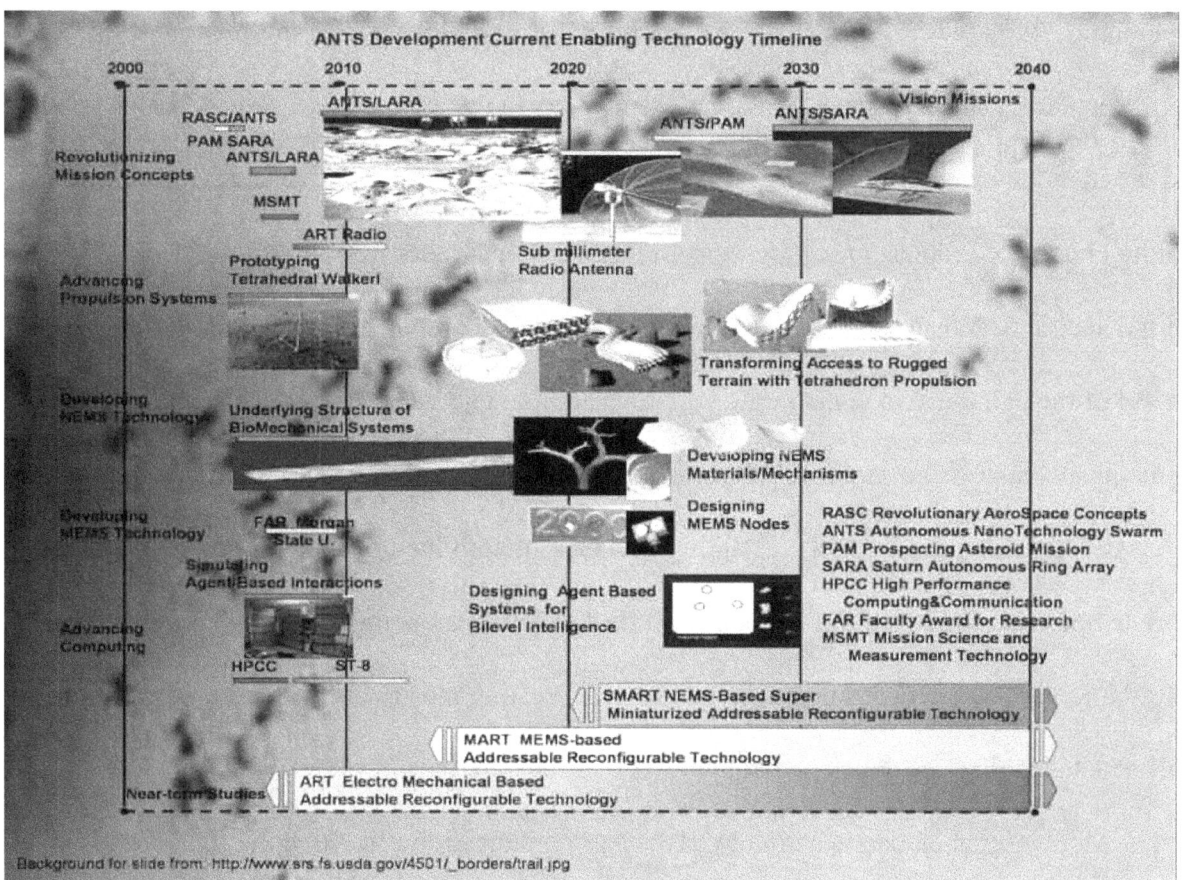

Figure 2. Autonmous NanoTechnology Swarms (ANTS) Development Timeline (reprinted from
http://ants.gsfc.nasa.gov/time.html).

Autonmous NanoTechnology Swarms (ANTS) is currently being researched by Goddard

Space Flight Center.[74] Modeled after insects, ANTS is network architecture applicable to future

nanofactories. Goddard Space Flight Center is currently using ANTS beginnings in experiments with large scale robot "herds." ANTS is the support structure for Addressable Reconfigurable Technology (ART). The core of ART is a networked swarm of nanomachines capable of configuring themselves for a variety of tasks.[75] The element control requirements for ARTs are nearly identical to what is required for the proposed network of nano-enabled balloons for weather sensing and control. The timeline of ANTS development in Figure 2 indicates usable functionality for distributed SANET control by 2030.

The individual methods of atmospheric modification at the molecular level share development with the capabilities of nanomachines. A combination of nano-pumps working at the molecular level can transport water between layers in the atmosphere as the balloons bob up and down in the air column.[76] Nanofactories can conduct electrolysis on water, molecularly building nuclei of droplets or ice crystals or reducing water vapor. Cooling through thermoelectric nanomaterials currently being designed for computer applications will enable control of the balloon skin temperature.[77, 78] This cooling and vapor content will have an effect on the localized pressure as a result of the ideal gas law. As with many non-linear systems, small inputs can develop large and self sustaining events, as determined by a 4d-Var model. Larger, more temperature based control balloons will be the center of the high and low pressure perturbations. The effect required is not as specific, resting mostly on regional temperature.[79] Will nanotechnology be developed to the level of atmospheric control by 2030?

Money spent on nanotechnology gives a good indication if it will continue to develop. Lux Research, a market science and economic research firm, claims that nanotechnology will become commonplace in across the spectrum of consumer goods by 2014.[80] 2004 showed a mere 12 million dollars invested globally in nanotechnology. In contrast, 2008 Lux Research estimates rise to 150 billion in sales of emerging nanotechnology. It is expected that sales of nanotechnology will reach 2.5 trillion dollars by 2014.[81] Dr. Hall, stated that "2030 nanotech is

24

likely to be good enough for a Weather Machine" in correspondence with the researcher.[82] Four generations of nanotechnology have been described by the U.S. National Nanotechnology Initiative (Fig 3).[83] We are currently in the second generation, specifically marked by the advances in computer CPU technology. Advances in the third generation will allow for much of the diamond nano-skinned balloon systems to function. The fourth generation will converge networkability, energy conversion and molecular scale activities in atmospheric change.[84]

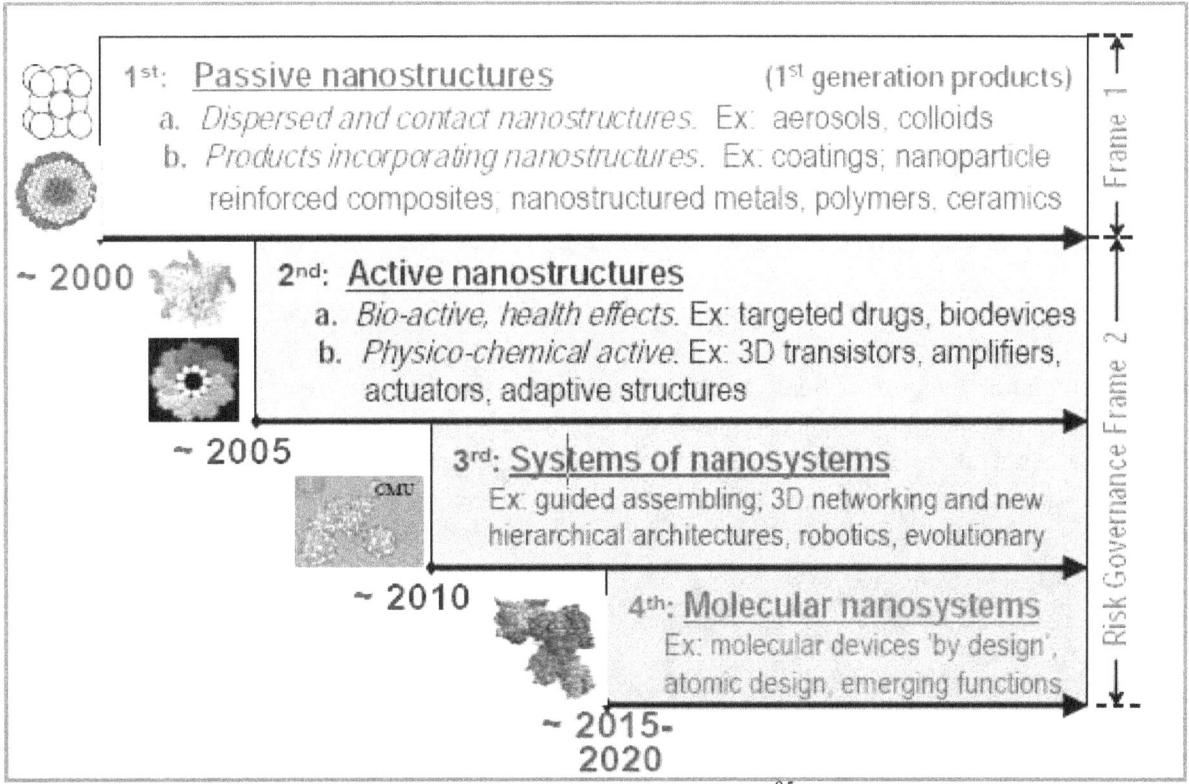

Figure 3. Four Generations of Nanotechnology Development.[85] (reprinted from "National Nanotechnology Initiative – Past Present and Future," http://www.nano.gov).

Nanotechnology enables the two critical humps in weather control. By the 2030 timeframe, nanotechnology will allow complex models to receive accurate and timely data from within and across the atmospheric system. These models can then direct those elements to make changes to the atmospheric system. System detail, data and response will be a function of the size of an area, how quickly it is changing and how many weather balloons are at your disposal.

Conclusion and Recommendations

The future of nanotechnology will enable creation of stratus cloud formations to defeat DEW and optically targeted attacks on United States assets. This research has shown that optical or directed energy systems can be rendered ineffective with clouds or dense fog. Clouds, rather than "smart dust" or ablative particle methods result in a persistent, regenerative defense against DEW. Advances in technology are beginning to bring weather phenomena more completely under our control. Current capabilities such as 4d-VAR computer modeling enable the establishment and design of a cloud system. Small diamond nano-skinned balloons allow the measurement and delivery devices to become elements of the weather system, removing closed-loop control response lag time. Nanotechnology allows these balloons to maneuver and network within and from the atmospheric system. Finally, nanotechnology facilitates the basic functions of measuring and changing critical variables required for weather control operations.

Concepts not covered in this research include the logistics of manning and operating a weather control system. Studying the requirements to support the span of technological systems and broad physical area will be necessary as weather control becomes a reality. The vulnerability or exploitive possibilities of the system can be analyzed in the process of developing tactics, techniques and procedures (TTPs) as with any major weapon system. Defense of a weather control system requires more specific details on the subsystems to be of use. Although described as a defensive measure in this project, the author fully realizes a wide spectrum of possible weather control applications. While conducting the environmental scan for this project many experts highlighted dangerous second and third order effects along with international opinion and law in regards to weather modification. In order to sustain a weather shield, other areas will have prolonged periods of perturbations. Although not a direct area of this particular paper, potential chain reactions and affects outside the specific area must be

26

considered an implemented into the Weather Operations Plan (WOP). The most important

recommendation is to begin monitoring and preparation for weather control technology.

Weather operators and organizations in the USAF need to monitor the technologies linked in this

discussion. As the capabilities converge, USAF organizations may be the key to engaging,

organizing and implementing the defensive use of weather control.

Appendix A: Concept Weather Control Relevance Tree

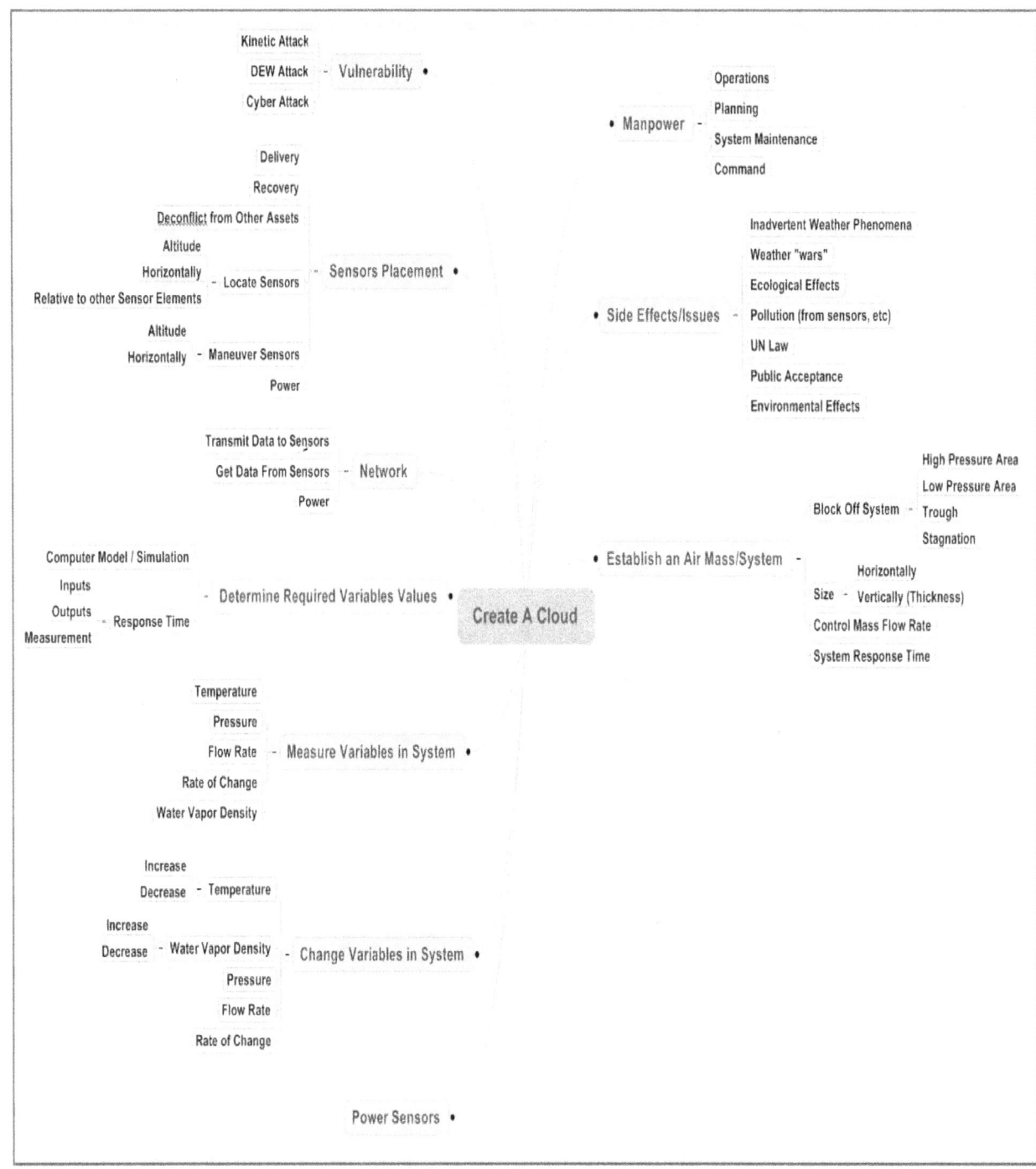

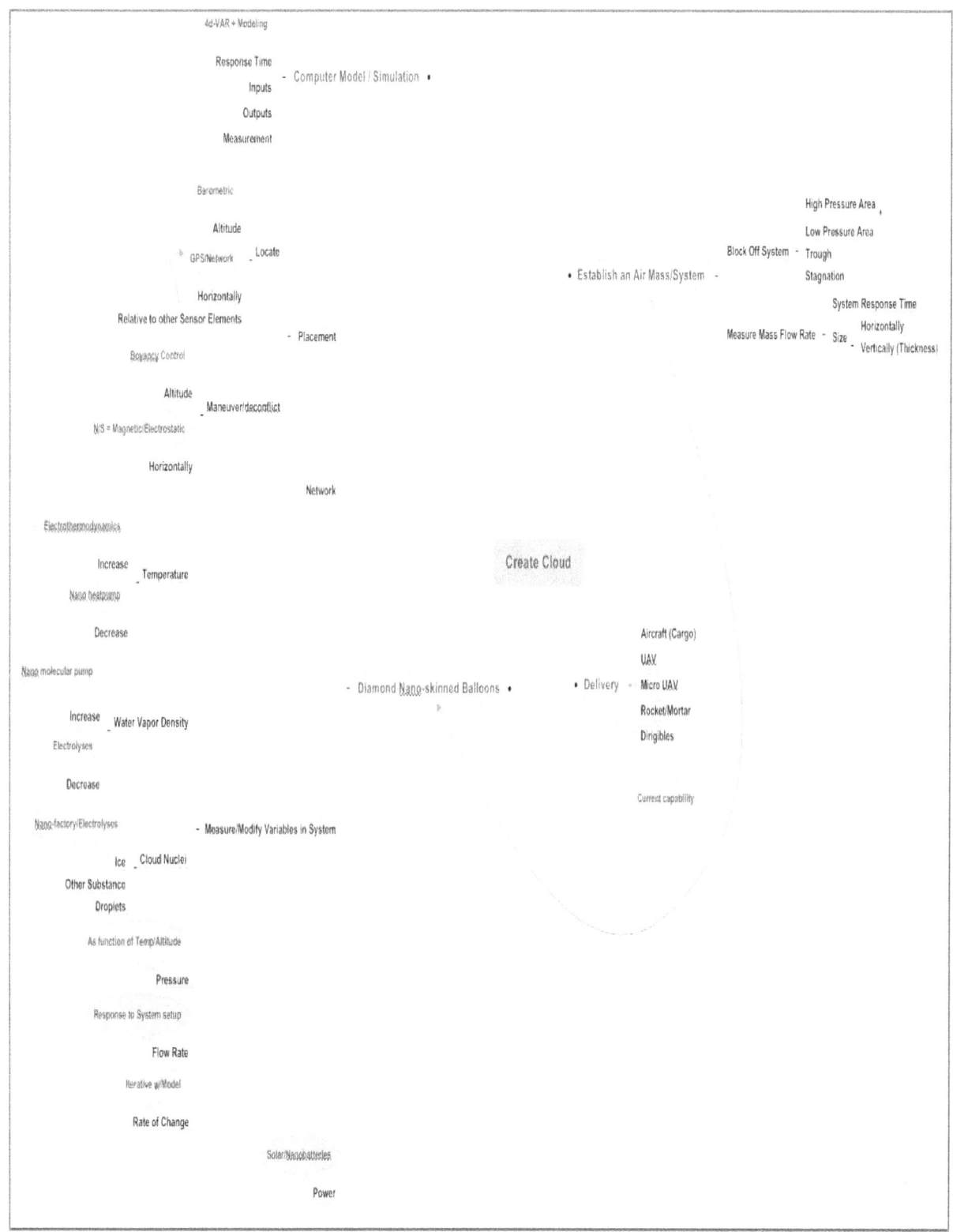

Appendix C: Acronym List

3d-Var – Three dimensional variation

4d-Var - Four dimensional variation

AGL – Above Ground Level

AAA – Anti-Aircraft Artillery

ANTS - Autonomous NanoTechnology Swarm

AOR - Area Of Regard

ART – Addressable Reconfigurable Technology

C2 – Command and Control

CFACC – Combined Forces Air Component Commander

CPU – Central Processing Unit

DE – Directed Energy

DEW – Directed Energy Weapon

DOD – Department of Defense

DWC – Defense Weather Command

EMP – Electro-Magnetic Pulse

FEBA – Forward Edge of the Battle Area

GHz - GigaHerz

HEL – High Energy Laser

HPM – High Power Microwave

IADS – Integrated Air Defense System

IR - InfraRed

ISR – Intelligence Surveillance and Reconnaissance

MSL – Mean Sea Level

NOAA – National Oceanic and Atmospheric Administration

NCAR - National Center for Atmospheric Research

PEM – Proton Exchange Membrane

SAM – Surface to Air Missile

SME – Subject Matter Expert

TOF – Time of Fall or Time of Flight

TTP – Tactics, Techniques and Procedures

UAV – Unmanned Aerial Vehicle

USAF – United States Air Force

UV – Ultra Violet

WMA – Weather Modification Assocation

WOP – Weather Operations Plan

WRFM – Weather Research and Forcasting Model

ENDNOTES

[1] Geis, "Directed Energy Weapons On The Battlefield: A New Vision For 2025", 1.

[2] Author's combat and planning.

[3] Thill, "Penetrating The Ion Curtain: Implications of Directed Energy Integrated Air Defense Systems in 2030", 7.

[4] Office of the Under Secretary of Defense for Acquisition, Technology and Logistics, *Defense Science Board Task Force on Directed Energy Weapons,* 20.

[5] National Research Council, *Critical Issues In Weather Modification Research,* 31-33.

[6] National Research Council, *Critical Issues In Weather Modification Research,* 23.

[7] William Langewieshe, "Stealing Weather," 172.

[8] Carlotti, "Two-point properties of atmospheric turbulence very close to the ground: Comparison of a high resolution LES with theoretical models."

[9] Volkovitsky, *Propigation of Intensive Laser Radiation in Clouds,* 8.

[10] Author's experience with F-16 optical and IR targeting systems

[11] http://www.satimagingcorp.com/satellite-sensors/geoeye-1.html

[12] http://www.tech-faq.com/low-earth-orbit.shtml

[13] http://www.satimagingcorp.com/satellite-sensors/geoeye-1.html

[14] Authors experience in the employment of UAV kinetic weapons

[15] Geis, "Directed Energy Weapons On The Battlefield: A New Vision For 2025", 1.

[16] Defense Science Board Task Board Report on Directed Energy Weapons, Memorandum For Chairman, Defense Science Board.

[17] Thill, "Penetrating The Ion Curtain: Implications of Directed Energy Integrated Air Defense Systems in 2030", 12.

[18] Thill, "Penetrating The Ion Curtain: Implications of Directed Energy Integrated Air Defense Systems in 2030", 10.

[19] Volkovitsky, *Propigation of Intensive Laser Radiation in Clouds,* 301.

[20] Volkovitsky*, Propigation of Intensive Laser Radiation in Clouds,* 18.

[21] Defense Science Board Task Board Report on Directed Energy Weapons, p ix.

[22] Thill, "Penetrating The Ion Curtain: Implications of Directed Energy Integrated Air Defense Systems in 2030", 9.

[23] Mueller, "The Relative Effects of CW and RP Lasers on Composites and Metals," 10, 13.

[24] http://hyperphysics.phy-astr.gsu.edu/Hbase/phyopt/grating.html#c1

[25] Reed, "Refraction of Light." http://www.ps.missouri.edu/rickspage/refract/refraction.html

[26] Volkovitsky, *Propigation of Intensive Laser Radiation in Clouds,* 16.

[27] Thill, "Penetrating The Ion Curtain: Implications of Directed Energy Integrated Air Defense Systems in 2030", 37.

[28] Allen, Uthe, "Tactical Considerations of Atmospheric Effects on Laser Propagation", p 12.

[29] Volkovitsky, *Propigation of Intensive Laser Radiation in Clouds,* 27.

[30] Kopp, "Beam Propagation", http://www.ausairpower.net/AADR-HEL-Dec-81.html.

[31] Volkovitsky, *Propigation of Intensive Laser Radiation in Clouds,* 200.

[32] HPM anti-personnel system demonstrated to Author while stationed at Moody AFB, GA.

[33] Thill, "Penetrating The Ion Curtain: Implications of Directed Energy Integrated Air Defense Systems in 2030", 11.

[34] Defense Science Board Task Board Report on Directed Energy Weapons, Memorandum For Chairman, Defense Science Board. p 35 – 36.

[35] Thill, "Penetrating The Ion Curtain: Implications of Directed Energy Integrated Air Defense Systems in 2030", 10.

[36] Narcisse, *Air Force Weather Preparations to Support Directed Energy Weapons Across the Department of Defense.* p 9.

[37] Thill, "Penetrating The Ion Curtain: Implications of Directed Energy Integrated Air Defense Systems in 2030", 10.

[38] Barry B. Coble, *Benign Weather Modification,* 9.

[39] Lewis, "Controlling the Weather"

[40] Howe, *The Need For Increased Control of Weather Modification Activities,* 23.

[41] National Research Council, *Critical Issues In Weather Modification Research,* 17.

[42] National Research Council, *Critical Issues In Weather Modification Research,* 18.

[43] Garstang, "Weather Modification, Finding Common Ground." 649-650.

[44] Klemp and Skamarock, *A Time-split Nonhydrostatic Atmospheric Model for Weather Research and Forecasting Applications,* p 2.

[45] National Research Council, *Critical Issues In Weather Modification Research,* 46.

[46] National Research Council, *Critical Issues In Weather Modification Research,* 30-33.

[47] Garstang, "Weather Modification, Finding Common Ground", 651.

[48] Weather Research and Forecasting Model, http://www.wrf-model.org/index.php

[49] "Final Report of the Technical Workshop on WRF-ESMF Convergence." http://www.wrf-model.org/wrfadmin/publications/WRF-ESMF-Convergence-Workshop.pdf.

[50] Skamarock, *A Time-split Nonhydrostatic Atmospheric Model for Weather Research and Forecasting Applications,* 4.

[51] Correspondence with William Shamarock, National Center for Atmospheric Research, 8 Dec 2008.

[52] Dr. Thomas DeFelice, Public Information Chairman of Weather Modification Association (WMA), NOAA contract manager and expert witness for Joint Hearing by Senate Subcommittee on Science & Space and Subcommittee on Disaster Prediction and Prevention, November 10, 2005.

Mr. Peter Backlund, National Center for Atmospheric Research (National Science Foundation) Director if Integrated Science Program and Research Relations

Dr. Ross Hoffman, Vice President, Research and Development of Atmospheric and Evironmental Research Inc, formerly with the NASA Institute for Advanced Concepts (NIAC).

Individual correspondence with six members of the Weather Modification Association. These members range from two weather PhD University professors and current weather modification industry representatives. Each member provided their inputs to both the concept and component relevance trees in the appendix of this paper. Since the accomplishment of the relevance trees, each of the six members independently requested that they not be directly associated with a military paper based on discrete weather control.

[53] Hoffman, *Controlling the Global Weather,* 3.

[54] Hoffman, *Controlling the Global Weather,* 4.

[55] Hoffman, *Controlling the Global Weather,* 1.

[56] Hoffman, *Controlling the Global Weather,* 6.

[57] Hoffman, *Controlling the Global Weather*, 3.

[58] Hoffman, *Controlling the Global Weather*, 5.

[59] Hoffman, *Controlling the Global Weather,* 3 and correspondence with Dr. Ross N. Hoffman.

[60] Hall, "The Weather Machine: Nano-enabled Climate Control for the Earth"

[61] Hall, "The Weather Machine: Nano-enabled Climate Control for the Earth"

[62] "Nano-Lightning Cooling For Computers," discussion of micro-scale ion-driven airflow, http://www.azonano.com/news.asp?newsID=68

[63] Ahmad, "Future Trends For Nanotechnology and the Application of Nanotechnology in Solar Cells, Nanofibres, Sensors, Ultra Light Materials and Corrosion Prevention," http://www.azonano.com/Details.asp?ArticleID=1718

[64] Kwok, "Felxible Nanoantenna Arrays Capture Abundant Solar Energy," http://www.eurekalert.org/pub_releases/2008-08/dnl-fna080808.php

[65] Hall, *Nanofuture, What's Next for Nanotechnology.* 53.

[66] Service, "TR10: NanRadio," http://www.technologyreview.com/communications/20244/

[67] Hall, "The Weather Machine: Nano-enabled Climate Control for the Earth"

[68] Correspondence with Dr. J. Storrs Hall.

[69] Dressler, *Self-Organization in Sensor and Actor Networks*, 6.

[70] Dressler, *Self-Organization in Sensor and Actor Networks*, 3.

[71] Dressler, *Self-Organization in Sensor and Actor Networks*, 9.

[72] Dressler, *Self-Organization in Sensor and Actor Networks*, 11,12.

[73] Dressler, *Self-Organization in Sensor and Actor Networks*, 10.

[74] http://ants.gsfc.nasa.gov/

[75] http://ants.gsfc.nasa.gov/ArchandAI.html

[76] Hall, *Nanofuture, What's Next for Nanotechnology,* 86.

[77] Correspondence with Dr. J. Storrs Hall

[78] Chowdhury, "On-Chip Cooling by Superlattice-based Thin-film Thermoelectics," http://www.nature.com/nnano/journal/vaop/ncurrent/abs/nnano.2008.417.html

[79] Correspondence with Dr. Ross N. Hoffman.

[80] "Statement of Findings: Sizing Nanotechnology's Value Chain," http://www.altassets.com/pdfs/sizingnanotechnologysvaluechain.pdf.

[81] "Statement of Findings: Sizing Nanotechnology's Value Chain," http://www.altassets.com/pdfs/sizingnanotechnologysvaluechain.pdf.

[82] Correspondence with Dr. J. Storrs Hall

[83] Roco, *National Nanotechnoloy Initiative – Past, Present, and Future.* 29.

[84] Roco, *National Nanotechnoloy Initiative – Past, Present, and Future.* 29.

[85] Roco, *National Nanotechnoloy Initiative – Past, Present, and Future.* 28.

BIBLIOGRAPHY

"Statement of Findings: Sizing Nanotechnology's Value Chain," Lux Research Inc. NY (2004). http://www.altassets.com/pdfs/sizingnanotechnologysvaluechain.pdf

A to Z of Nanotechnology. "Nano-Lightning Cooling For Computers." http://www.azonano.com/news.asp?newsID=68

Ahmad, Zaki. A to Z of Nanotechnology. "Future Trends For Nanotechnology and the Application of Nanotechnology in Solar Cells, Nanofibres, Sensors, Ultra Light Materials and Corrosion Prevention." http://www.azonano.com/Details.asp?ArticleID=1718

Allen, Robert, Edward Uthe, *Tactical Considerations of Atmospheric Effects on Laser Propagation.* Ft Belboir, VA: Defense Technical Information Center, Feb 1968Berube,

David M. *Nano-Hype, The Truth Behind The Nanotechnology Buzz.* Prometheus Books, New York 2006.

Breuer, Georg. *Weather Modification: Prospects and Problems*. Cambridge University Press, London, 1979.

Carlotti, Pierre. Two-Point Properties of Atmospheric Turbulence Very Close To The Ground: Comparison Of A High Resolution LES With Theoretical Models," *Boundary-Layer Meteorology* no. 104 (September 2002): 381-410.

Center for Embedded Network Sensing. "What is Embedded Network Sensing?" http://research.cens.ucla.edu/about/whatisens

Chowdhury, Ihtesham, Ravi Prasher, Kelly Lofgreen, et all, "On-Chip Cooling by Superlattice-based Thin-film Thermoelectics." *Nature Nanotechnology* (January 2009).

Coble, Barry B. "Benign Weather Modification." *USAF School of Advanced Airpower Studies*, Air University, Maxwell AFB, AL, March 1997.

Coila,Bridget. "Changing the Weather." *Weatherwise,* Vol 3, Issue 58 (May/June 2005):50-54.

Committee on the Status and Future Directions in U.S Weather Modification Research and Operations, National Research Council. *Critical Issues in Weather Modification Research.* The National Academies Press, Washington D.C. *2003.*

Defense Science Board Task Force on Directed Energy Weapons. Office of the Under Secretary of Defense for Acquisition, Technology and Logistics, December 2007.

Dressler, Falko. *Self-Organization in Sensor and Actor Networks.* John Wiley and Sons, 2007.

Garstang, Michael, Roelof Bruintjes, Robert Seragin, Harold Orville, Bruce Boe, William

Cotton, Joseph Warburton. "Weather Modification, Finding Common Ground." *Bulletin of American Meteorological Society.* Vol 86, Issue 5 (May 2004): 647-655.

Geis, John P. II. "Directed Energy Weapons On The Battlefield: A New Vision For 2025" CSAT Occasional paper 32, Air University, Maxwell AFB, AL, April 2003.

Goddard Space Flight Center. "Autonomous Nantochnology Swarms: ANTS." http://ants.gsfc.nasa.gov/ArchandAI.html

Hall, J. Storrs. *Nanofuture, What's Next for Nanotechnology.* Prometheus Books, New York, 2005.

Hall, J. Storrs. *The Weather Machine: Nano-enabled Climate Control for the Earth.* Global Catastrophic Risks 2008 Conference Video. 15 min., 2008. Web Video: http://www.vimeo.com/2539563

Hoffman Ross N. *Controlling the Global Weather.* USRA and NIAC final report, March 2004.

Howe, George W. *The Need For Increased Control of Weather Modification Activities.* Air Univesity, Maxwell AFB, AL, 1973.

House, Tamzy J. et al. "Weather as a Force Multiplier: Owning the Weather in 2025, Military Applications of Weather Modification." *Air Force 2025*, Maxwell AFB, AL, Augus 1996.

Kopp, Carlo. "Beam Propagation." *Australian Aviation & Defense Review Dec 1981.* http://www.ausairpower.net/AADR-HEL-Dec-81.html. (accessed 12 Jan 09).

Kwok, Roberta, "Flexible Nanoantenna Arrays Capture Abundante Solar Energy," *American Association for the Advancement of Science EurekAlert Aug 2008.* http://www.eurekalert.org/pub_releases/2008-08/dnl-fna080808.php#. (accessed 18 Jan 09)

Leonard David. "U.S. Military Wants to Own the Weather," Space.com, 31 Oct 2005. http://www.space.com/scienceastronomy/051031_mystery_monday.html

Lewis, Amy, "Controlling the Weather."http://www.weather.com/newscenter/atmospheres/feature/091300feature.html, Sept 2000

List, Roland. "'Scientific Proof' in Weather Modification." *Bulletin of the American Meteorological Society*, Vol 86, Issue 11 (Nov 2005): 1527-1530.

List, Roland. "Weather Modification – A Scenario for the Future," *Bulletin of the American Meteorological Society*, Vol 85, Issue 1 (Jan 2004): 51-64.

Mueller, George. "The Relative Effects of CW and RP Lasers on Composites and Metals."

Directed Energy Effects Branch, Condensed Matter and Radiation Division, Naval Research Laboratories, 7 September 1995. http://www.dtic.mil/cgi-bin/GetTRDoc?AD=ADA299524&Location=U2&doc=GetTRDoc.pdf

Narcisse, De Leon. "Air Force Weather Preparations to Support Directed Energy Weapons Across the Department of Defense." Air University, Maxwell AFB, AL, April 2007.

Optical and Laser Effects. "Diffraction Grating." http://hyperphysics.phy-astr.gsu.edu /Hbase/phyopt/grating.html#c1

Reed, Rick. "Refraction of Light." http://www.ps.missouri.edu/rickspage/refract/refraction.html.

Roco, M.C. "National Nanotechnoloy Initiative – Past, Present, and Future." *Handbook on Nanoscience, Engineering and Technology, 2nd ed.* National Science Foundation and National Nanotechnology Initiative. February 2006.

Satellite Imaging Corporation. "GEOEYE-1 Satellite Imagery/Sensor Specifications. http://www.satimagingcorp.com/satellite-sensors/geoeye-1.html.

Service, Robert. "TR10: NanoRadio." *Technology Review March/April 2008.* http://www.technologyreview.com/communications/20244/. (accessed 15 Feb 2009).

Skamarock, William, Joseph Kemp. "A Time-Split Nonhydrostatic Atmospheric Model for Weather Research and Forcasting Applications." *Journal of Computational Physics.* National Center for Atmospheric Research, Boulder Co. (July 2006).

TechFAQ. "What is Low Earth Orbit?" http://www.tech-faq.com/low-earth-orbit.shtml

The Weather Research & Forcasting Model. http://wrf-model.org/index.php.

The Weather Research & Forcasting Model. "Final Report of the Technical Workshop on WRF-ESMF Convergence." http://www.wrf-model.org/wrfadmin/publications/WRF-ESMF-Convergence-Workshop.pdf, Feb 2006.

Thill, Joseph A. "Penetrating The Ion Curtain: Implications of Directed Energy Integrated Air Defense Systems in 2030." Air University, Maxwell AFB, AL, April 2008.

Volkovitsky, Oleg, Yuri Sedunov and Leonid Semonov. *Propigation of Intensive Laser Radiation in Clouds.* Reston: American Institute of Aeronautics & Astronautics, 1992.

William Langewieshe, "Stealing Weather," *Vanity Fair*, May 2008, 172.